Sally's gifts as an author and educator come to life in her new Children's Devotional which is based on core Biblical truths and the values of Christianity.

She uses child-friendly concepts and language to practically guide your child to change from a hearer of the word to a doer of the word!

While each devotional is based on a scripture and contains a rich practical application of a story in Sally's 9-part series of Sarah's Amazing Animal Adventures, these devotionals move far beyond the stories.

Your child will not only be instructed in scripture, but then be given an opportunity to apply the lessons into his/her everyday life through completing an external meaningful activity to take action and then internalize the reading through a guided prayer. Do not miss out on this outstanding opportunity to raise godly children.

Jeanette Edwards, Educator

Paul wrote to young Timothy: "Don't have anything to do with godless stories and silly tales. Instead, train yourself to be godly. Training the body has some value. But being godly has value in every way. It promises help for the life you are now living and the life to come." I Timothy 4:7-8

Sally's stories, workbooks and this devotional help me and my daughter, Jubilee, abide by Paul's teaching. They are wonderful and welcomed supplements,

helping me and so many others provide godly instruction to our young while keeping them engaged, and the morals we wish to teach relatable to the relationships and situations they encounter in life.

This devotional is just another huge blessing in our library. Thank you, Sally Betters and Mary Jane Lopez. I appreciate and applaud your efforts towards providing meaningful and instructional materials for children that give great lessons in life, love, and leadership all while pointing to God, our guide, provider, and sustainer.

Michelle Wright, Parent

What a fantastic devotional for children that follows Sarah's Amazing Animal Adventures book series! This devotional is perfect for young children to learn more about being a friend, obeying, kindness, compassion, and so many amazing biblical principles. As a teacher and mother of two, I love the activity section of this devotional because it allows children to self-reflect and speak to God in a short prayer. This devotional can also be enjoyed as a family, and the activities can be discussed during dinnertime or even car rides!

Elizabeth Avveduto,
Parent and Elementary School Instructor

This children's devotional helps children relate scripture to real-life experiences through Sarah's adventures. It gives children simple prayers to use while strengthening their relationship with Jesus.

Parents, this will be a great resource to begin conversations with your children about living a faith-based life.

Amy Ambrozich, M.A.,
Certified Parenting and Stepfamily Coach
http://www.daretoparent.com/

Gregory the Great wrote, "Scripture is like a river again, broad and deep, shallow enough here for the lamb to go wading, but deep enough there for the elephant to swim." Often, lambs struggle wading out into a river and become confused or frightened. Sarah, the main character in this collection of stories, lovingly cares for and serves her canine friends as she helps them navigate troubled waters. In the same way, we can help Christ's little lambs wade out into the water of God's Word through this collection of stories by Sally Betters. Each story takes a deeply profound Gospel truth and expresses it in ways that even a child can grasp through a story, an activity, and a prayer for God's leading through various situations.

Vance Salisbury, Author, *"Good Mr. Baxter: Sketches of Effective Gospel-centered Leadership from the Life of Richard Baxter"*

The Amazing Adventures Continue: A Walk With Jesus

A Children's Devotional Companion to the Series

SALLY BETTERS

WITH MARY JANE LOPEZ

Illustrated by Linda Lloyd

.

Book Design & Production by Lynn Caprarelli
ISBN: 9798409937102

DEDICATIONS

To children young and old who desire an amazing
adventure with Jesus.

~ Sally Betters

To my youngest twin granddaughters, Aubrey and
Kinsley. May you grow to love the Lord with all your
heart, soul, mind, and strength.

~Mary Jane Lopez

May the words and illustrations of this book reach
those little ones whom God loves and keeps watch
over.

~Linda Lloyd

SPECIAL THANKS

I want to extend a wholehearted thank you to the following devoted family and friends. My heart is full with your generous gestures of kindness, skills and talents. Your prayers, donations and words of encouragement are a valuable part of this book.

Richard Betters, Edmund N. Sanchez, Arcy Torres, Arcy Piña, Dr. Edward Piña, Willa Gardea, Mary Jane López, Steve López, Linda Lloyd, Kathy Cox, Kathy Johnson, Anita M. McLaurin, Nanette O'Neal, Traci Harris, Dan Broyles, Linda and James Mendel, Carole Boersma, Jeanette Edwards, Julie Ann Cooper, Roberta Bryer-King, Renee Vidor, Peggy Hinman, Michael and Kristine Freedman, Pat Weaver, and Lynn Caprarelli

INTRODUCTION

This Children's Devotional, *The Amazing Adventures Continue: A Walk With Jesus* is a valued addition to the *Sarah's Amazing Animal Adventures* series.

Each devotional is taken from the character themes in the Sarah books. They are uniquely designed to invite a child into a genuine and personal relationship with his/her creator, God.

A supporting scripture begins each devotional, followed by an activity to help process the practical aspect of the lesson. Finally, each devotional passage concludes with a simple prayer to summarize a child's request to God about that particular message.

Author Sally Betters created *Sarah's Amazing Animal Adventures*: *A Series of Children's Stories about Character Displayed Through Love and Kindness* to provide readers with character building and value-based learning. All proceeds of her books, speaking, and life coaching support ZOE International, an international non-profit organization active in five countries providing prevention, rescue, and restoration to youth caught in the web of child sex trafficking.

Mary Jane Lopez makes her debut as a gifted co-author in this heartwarming children's compass, which points to a strong relationship with Jesus Christ. Mrs. Lopez brings her talent and experience writing devotionals for her church newsletter and administrative skills from her many years working for a school district.

"Let the children come to me, and do not hinder them, for to such belongs the kingdom of God. Truly, I say to you, whoever does not receive the kingdom of God like a child shall not enter it."

Luke 18:16

TABLE OF CONTENTS

Book 1 – Sarah's Dream Comes True 2

Book 2 – Sarah Helps Roman Find His Forever Home 15

Book 3 – Sarah Teaches Daisy Her True Beauty 22

Book 4 – Reunited 31

Book 5 – Memories and Losses 42

Book 6 – Taking Care of Loved Ones 61

Book 7 – New Beginnings 69

Book 8 – Dog Jackets And The Unexpected 77

Book 9 – Joseph's Secret 84

SARAH'S Amazing ANIMAL ADVENTURES

A Series of Children's Stories About Character
Displayed Through Love and Kindness

Book ONE

SARAH'S DREAM COMES TRUE

SALLY BETTERS
Illustrated by Linda Lloyd

Book 1 - Sarah's Dream Comes True

"A friend loveth at all times..."

Proverbs 17:17 KJV

Do you long for a friend? Maybe you're an only child like Sarah, or maybe you are shy and find it hard to make friends. If we want to have friends, we need to learn how to be a friend.

Sarah was lonely. She longed for a pet as much as she longed for a friend. Sometimes God uses our pets to teach us how to be a friend. We learn to love our pets and look after them. When they want our attention, we are quick to respond. Although they don't talk to us like Sarah's pet, we often talk to our pets, and they show us affection and give us companionship. We learn to love and protect them. They become our friends and part of our family.

Having a human friend to talk with is terrific—a friend who listens to us and helps us not feel lonely. And we learn to listen to them and get to know what they like and don't like. But a friend can't be with us every minute of the day, except for one friend: His name is Jesus! He is not imaginary. He is real, and though he lives in Heaven, He can also live in our hearts. He watches over us, He listens to us when we pray, and He even promises never to leave us. He loves us "at all times."

Jesus can live in your heart, all you have to do is ask Him, and He will be your forever friend.

ACTIVITY

Ask Jesus to come into your heart so He can be your faithful friend. Then talk with your mom and dad and tell them that you want Jesus as your lifetime friend and companion.

PRAYER

Dear Jesus, thank you for loving me and telling me you will never leave me. Please come into my heart so I will never be alone. Teach me how to be a good friend to others. Amen.

"Children, obey your parents in all things, for this is well-pleasing in the Lord."

Colossians 3:20 ASV

One of the first things God wants us to do when we ask Jesus into our heart is love Him with all our heart, mind, soul, and strength. This is called a commandment. So how do we do that?

One way is to obey our parents. The Bible says that this act of respect pleases the Lord. When something is pleasing to God, it means that it makes Him happy. It shows our love for Him and our parents.

Sarah wasn't happy when her parents told her she wasn't ready for a pet. She was sad. It may have even made her a little angry. There isn't anything wrong with being sad or angry, but sometimes we can show our unhappiness in how we behave.

How do you behave when your parents don't, or can't, give you what you want? Do you cry? Do you throw things? Do you yell or say mean things to them?

God wants us to obey our parents in all things. That means that even if we are sad or mad, we should not do or say something we might be sorry for later.

Sarah may have cried, and she may have been angry at times. But one thing we know for sure is that Sarah prayed. She prayed to Jesus. She knew Jesus was her friend, and He would listen; we must also learn to listen to Jesus and obey our parents. He knows what's best for us, and so do our parents.

🐾 ACTIVITY

Is there something you have done that you want to apologize for to your mom, dad, sister, brother, or friend? We all make mistakes and feel better when we say we are sorry, so there are no bad or sad feelings between the people we care about and us.

🐾 PRAYER

Dear Jesus, thank you for giving me a mom and dad (or grandparents) who love me. Teach me how to obey them by not misbehaving when I don't get my way. Teach me to please You by pleasing them. Amen.

*"Every good gift and every perfect gift is from above
and comes down from the Father of lights...."*
James 1:17 ESV

What do you think of when you think of a gift? I think
of a box wrapped in bright paper with a fluffy bow on
top or a colorful bag filled with tissue paper. Inside is a
surprise! Opening the package is like unraveling a
mystery! You may discover something fun, something
you need, or something you've wished and hoped for
and maybe even prayed about for a long time.

Can you imagine Sarah's excitement when she
opened her Christmas gift? It was probably the best gift
she had ever received. It was perfect!

But have you ever thought about the person who
gave you the gift? Was it a friend or a family member?
Usually, those who know and love us have a good idea
about what gifts will truly make our hearts happy.

Did you know that there is someone who knows us
better than anyone? Remember His name? It's Jesus!
He is our gift, and He loves us so much and knows us so
well that he can even help our parents decide if, or
when, they should give us something we ask for. And
like our parents, He doesn't always give us what we
want, when we want it, because it may not be what's
best for us at the time.

Sarah had to wait a little while for the pet she wanted, but she remained hopeful. Waiting isn't a bad thing. Most of the time, it's a good thing, especially when a gift comes from our Father in heaven above. He gives good and perfect gifts at a good and perfect time because God is good and perfect. Our Father in heaven made us and knows everything about us! He even created heaven and earth, but most importantly, He created you.

ACTIVITY

Tell someone about a time when you had to wait for something you wanted. Let them know if it made you appreciate it more because you had to earn it.

PRAYER

Dear Jesus, thank you for being good and perfect. Thank you for loving me and wanting what's best for me. Teach me to trust you when I have to wait or don't get what I want. Show me how to take good care of the gifts I receive. Amen.

"See how very much our Father loves us, for he calls us his children, and that is what we are!"

1 John 3:1 NLT

Some children have large families. Some have small families. Some only have a mom or a dad, while others live with their grandma, grandpa, or aunt and uncle. We are born into those families.

Some special people are not family members but adopt and take care of those who may not have a family to love and protect them.

Sarah's dog, Sarge, was adopted. Sarah's family adopted Sarge so they could give him a safe and happy home.

The Bible says that when we believe in Jesus and welcome Him into our hearts, he adopts us, and we become part of His family.

Even if we already belong to a family, we can also become children of God, and all His children become our brothers and sisters in Christ.

Sarge was thankful to be adopted and belong to Sarah's family, and Sarah was thrilled to have Sarge in her life. Overjoyed is how God feels when we join His family, and thankful is how we feel when we belong to Jesus!

 ## ACTIVITY

Draw a picture or write a story of someone you know who is adopted. If you don't know someone who is adopted, then draw a picture of an adopted animal.

PRAYER

Dear Jesus, thank you for adopting me into your family because You love me. Show me how to love and care for others so that they can become part of your family too. Amen.

"Don't worry about anything; instead, pray about everything. Tell God what you need and thank him for all he has done. Then you will experience God's peace, which exceeds anything we can understand."

Philippians 4:6-7 NLT

We have all worried about something; perhaps a new school, making friends, homework, grades. We can worry about our family and our pets. Some worries are small, but they can grow into big concerns if we think about them too much. That's because we have active imaginations that can think of all sorts of complicated things. Worry can make us afraid.

When Sarge was taking care of his brother and sister, he had a lot to worry about; for example, where they would sleep and what they would eat.

How did Sarge handle his worry? He took action. Sarge didn't let anxiety or fear keep him from looking for food or finding a warm place to sleep for his siblings, and most importantly, Sarge remembered to pray! And, after he prayed, he thanked God and experienced God's peace.

God commands us NOT to worry or be afraid, and He tells us how to do that. We are to "pray about everything," "tell Him everything," and "thank him for everything He has already done." When we do these things, we will also experience God's peace, as Sarge did.

What does God's peace feel like? Sarge described it as 'a warm breeze.' God's peace can make us feel calm even when nothing around us is peaceful. It can make us feel as though everything is going to be ok. When God watches over us, He hears our prayers and calms our fears. Even if our prayers are not answered right away, we can still feel His peace. Our hearts know He's taking care of us. And, when we thank Him for what he's done for us, we are reminded of His faithfulness.

ACTIVITY

Sit down and write a list of good things God has done for you, and when you are worried or afraid, pray and remember His goodness. Tell Him everything and then wait for His peace to comfort you.

PRAYER

Dear God, thank you for taking care of my worries and fears. I'm grateful I can tell you everything! Help me to remember all the good things you've done for me so that I won't doubt you. Help me to experience Your peace. Amen.

"...remember the words of the Lord Jesus, that he himself said, It is more blessed to give than to receive."
Acts 20:35 ASV

Like Sarah, we've all received gifts that delight us, but giving a gift can be even more exciting. Especially when we see the person's face light up when they receive our offering, we get to experience the joy with them!

Gifts don't have to cost money. A gift can be as simple as a wildflower you plucked from the ground and gave to someone. I'm pretty sure wildflowers are the first gifts most of us have given as children. As we grow, we discover there are many more ways to give gifts. We can buy a gift or give our time and effort by being helpful to others. Doing a chore around the house without being asked to do it can be considered a gift. We can even pray for or with someone.

When Sarah's parents felt it was time to give Sarah the pet she longed for, they were excited for her. They knew how happy she would be to open her surprise gift.

After Sarah learned what Sarge had been through and how he hoped to reunite with his brother and sister, it was now Sarah's turn to give her time and effort to help. First, she thanked her mom and dad and God for her gift, and then she eagerly determined in her heart to help her new friend, Sarge.

We can do the same. When we see others around us who may need a helping hand, a kind word, a prayer, or even a wildflower, stop to give them a gift of a smile, your help, your attention, or your time. And don't forget to tell them about Jesus! God promises you will be blessed.

ACTIVITY

Look for ways to bless others today. It may be a smile, a kind word, helping someone carry something, picking a flower for them, or drawing them a picture. There are so many ways to bring joy into someone's life.

PRAYER

Dear God, thank you for your promises. Thank you for your perfect gifts. You are a gift to me. Teach me to be a gift to others. Show me how to pray for those I love. Show me how to bless those around me with Your love and kindness. Amen.

SARAH'S Amazing ANIMAL ADVENTURES

A Series of Children's Stories About Character
Displayed Through Love and Kindness

Book Two

SARAH HELPS ROMAN FIND HIS FOREVER HOME

SALLY BETTERS
Illustrated by Linda Lloyd

Book 2 — Sarah Helps Roman Find His Forever Home

"So in everything, do to others what you would have them do to you…"

Matthew 7:12 NIV

The Golden Rule

Sarah loved Sarge so much that she was excited to take good care of him. However, after she heard his story about losing his family, she was filled with compassion.

Compassion is an emotion we feel when we see someone going through something difficult and we want to help them any way we can. We want to treat them the way we would like to be treated if we had the same problem. This is called 'The Golden Rule' - "Do unto others as you would have them do unto you."

Sarah could have easily ignored or forgotten about Sarge's troubles and yet continued to take good care of him, but she cared very deeply about how he felt, so instead, she made a decision to do something about it.

Next time you encounter someone who is having a bad day, a bad week, a bad time, think about how you might feel if it were happening to you, and "do unto others as you would have them do unto you."

🐾 ACTIVITY

Look for an opportunity to show compassion to someone who is hurting and give them a hug, write them a note, draw them a picture, or sing them a song.

🐾 PRAYER

Dear God, thank you for your compassion for Your children. Teach me to have Your compassion for others and treat them the way I want to be treated. Amen.

"But the Holy Spirit produces this kind of fruit in our lives: love, joy, peace, patience, kindness, goodness, faithfulness, gentleness, and self-control."

Galatians 5:22 NLT

Do you have a favorite fruit? Most fruit we eat is healthy, sweet, and grows on trees or vines. Fruit doesn't grow quickly. It takes time. It must be watered and tended to so it can mature and ripen to be ready to eat. It's very nutritious (good for you) and tastes delicious. Yum!

There is also another kind of fruit that God gives us when we follow Him. These are called the fruits of the Spirit because they come from the Holy Spirit who lives in us when we ask Jesus to come into our hearts. These fruits are special qualities that grow within us as we walk with God.

Both Sarah and Sarge have displayed many of these fruitful qualities: love, joy, and kindness, just to name a few. Can you think of which qualities are most evident?

Which fruit is God growing in your heart? God doesn't want to deprive you of any of these. On the contrary, he wants you to have them all. So, as you read His word and practice your faith, remember, the Holy Spirit will do the rest.

 ## ACTIVITY

Take a moment to think about what kind of fruit of the Spirit you may already have.

 ## PRAYER

Dear God, thank you for the fruit of the Spirit that represents who You are. I want You to grow the fruit of the Spirit in my heart. Amen.

"For we are God's masterpiece. He has created us anew in Christ Jesus so we can do the good things he planned for us long ago."

Ephesians 2:10 NLT

Have you ever made something with your hands? Maybe you drew a picture or molded something with clay. Did you give it to your mom, dad, grandparents, or teacher? Whatever you made, I know it was beautiful. It was a masterpiece! A unique work of art you created to bring joy to your loved ones.

Isn't it fantastic that God created us to be His masterpiece? We are each unique and beautiful in His eyes and individually designed for His specific purpose.

Daisy is a lovely, cheerful dog who loves sparkling bows and receives many compliments about her beauty. But she doesn't need the sparkling bows and compliments to know she's beautiful. She needs only to see herself through God's eyes. The One who created her to serve others and fulfill God's plan for her life.

ACTIVITY

Have you ever felt like Daisy did and needed something special to wear to feel special? Write about it in your journal or draw a picture of that event.

PRAYER

Dear God, thank you that I am your masterpiece. You designed me perfectly to fulfill Your plan. I pray that you would help me see myself through Your eyes to do the good things you have planned for me. Amen.

SARAH'S Amazing ANIMAL ADVENTURES

A Series of Children's Stories About Character
Displayed Through Love and Kindness

Book THREE

SARAH TEACHES DAISY HER TRUE BEAUTY

SALLY BETTERS
Illustrated by Linda Lloyd

Book 3 — Sarah Teaches Daisy Her True Beauty

"And why worry about your clothing? Look at the lilies of the field and how they grow."

Matthew 6:28 NLT

Daisy certainly loved dressing up. She had favorite vests and bows that made her feel pretty, and she received lots of attention when she wore them.

Most of us have favorite clothes that make us feel good. Maybe it's a new pair of shoes or a new shirt. When we wear it, we feel special, and we want others to notice us.

Some of us can't afford new things so we must wear the same clothes repeatedly. Of course, there's nothing wrong with that. At least we have clothes to wear. Imagine if we didn't!

God doesn't want us to overthink what we wear. Jesus Himself tells us not to worry about it. The One who created you also created the flowers of the field. And if God takes care of them and dresses them so splendidly, then how much more will He take care of you! So let your faith be in God and trust Him to take care of you.

✺ ACTIVITY

The next time you pick out what clothes you want to wear, stop and thank God for each item you have.

✺ PRAYER

Dear God, thank you for taking care of me and providing clothes for me to wear. Thank you that I am more important to you than flowers. You created me to shine so that others see You in me. And that's more special than any pair of new shoes. Amen.

"The Lord doesn't see things the way you see them. People judge by outward appearance, but the Lord looks at the heart."

1 Samuel 16:7 NLT

Daisy was learning a hard lesson. Her disappointment at not winning first place in the cutest dog contest showed that she was placing her faith in her outward appearance.

It's not that we shouldn't care how we look, but sometimes, when we don't take care of our appearance, it can draw unwanted attention. And we don't want that either. So instead, we should never forget how God sees us. He knows our hearts, and that's what matters - how we treat others.

ACTIVITY

Ask someone you are close to if you are loving, kind, and compassionate toward others. Is there an inward beauty that radiates outwardly and shines brightly so that you can attract others to Jesus?

PRAYER

Dear God, thank you that I am fearfully and wonderfully made. Your Word says so! Keep teaching me to be loving, kind, and compassionate toward others so that my outward appearance reflects my heart. Amen.

"Who shall separate us from the love of Christ?"
Romans 8:35 KJV

Daisy wanted to feel loved and accepted, but when she didn't win the contest, she thought she had lost everything. Sarah, Sarge, and Roman reassured her that she didn't need to win a competition for them to love her. She was special to them!

We want to be accepted by everyone around us, especially by our friends and family. Sometimes we don't feel loved at all. But we have a God whose love endures forever, and we are very special to Him. When we come to know and love God, He promises that nothing can separate us from His love! God is faithful and true even when things don't go our way, even when we are worried or afraid, even when we mess up.

ACTIVITY

Say this verse three times every day for a week until you have it memorized.

"Nothing shall be able to separate us from the love of God, which is in Christ Jesus our Lord." Romans 8:39 KJV

 ## PRAYER

Dear God, thank you for loving me and accepting me into your family. Thank you that Your promises are true. Help me remember that nothing can separate me from Your love even when I feel unloved, and everything seems to go wrong. Amen.

"Wait patiently for the Lord. Be brave and courageous. Yes, wait patiently for the Lord."

Psalms 27:14 NLT

It had been five years since Sarge, Daisy, and Roman last saw their parents, whom thieves had stolen. They had lost hope of ever seeing them again.

Sometimes we lose hope that our prayers will be answered. We all know that waiting is hard, and when we have to wait for something we want, it can seem like forever.

There is a song we sing in church that says, "Strength will rise as we wait upon the Lord..., Our God, our strong deliverer," and that is true!

Remember those fruits of the Spirit that God grows in us? Well, patience is one of them. When we are waiting for God's perfect timing, He is also growing the fruit of patience in us. Sometimes we have to be brave while we wait, and bravery takes strength and courage. Those are some great qualities to have, and when we rely on God, He delivers!

We must remember that the Lord does everything in His time, not ours because his timing is perfect.

Think about how brave Sarge had to be to take care of his siblings. Think about how much courage Sarah had to have to find their stolen parents.

Not all things turn out the way we would like them to. And over time, we may also realize that what we thought we wanted wasn't good for us. But one thing we can be sure of is this - anytime we wait on the Lord, we can trust Him to take care of us in His perfect way.

ACTIVITY

Share with someone close to you about a time when you were brave like Sarge.

PRAYER

Dear God, thank you that your timing is perfect. Thank you that when I wait on you, Lord, you give me strength and courage while You grow the fruit of patience in me. Amen.

SARAH'S Amazing ANIMAL ADVENTURES

A Series of Children's Stories About Character
Displayed Through Love and Kindness

Book FOUR

REUNITED

SALLY BETTERS
Illustrated by Linda Lloyd

Book 4 — Reunited

"In nothing be anxious, but in everything by prayer and supplication with thanksgiving let your requests be made known unto God."

Philippians 4:6 ASV

Anxious is kind of a big word to describe what Sarah felt when she found out that Sarge's mom and dad might be alive. She was so worried, she couldn't concentrate on school or even talk to her mom on the way to school. Yet she was excited and worried all at the same time.

God instructs us to "be anxious for nothing." That's right, NOTHING!

How do we do that when we can't help but worry about what might happen?

First of all, God doesn't leave us guessing about what to do. He tells us "in everything," (yes EVERYTHING, good or bad), to give all our requests to Him.

How? "By prayer and supplication" (uh oh, another big word); supplication means to be humble and sincere when we pray. He wants to be involved in every detail of our lives.

31

And last of all, He tells us to do it "with thanksgiving." Always be thankful to God. Thankful for what? Thankful that we can always go to Him and give our requests to Him because He gives us peace when we do. (Philippians 4:7, make sure to look this up in your Bible).

🐾 ACTIVITY

Write down five things you are thankful for in your journal.

🐾 PRAYER

Dear God, thank You that "in everything" I can pray humbly to you, and You promise to give me peace no matter what my troubles are. Amen.

"Commit thy works unto the LORD, and thy thoughts shall be established."

Proverbs 16:3 KJV

After Sarah had time to process the possibilities of finding Sarge's and his siblings' parents, she decided to ask God for guidance. She didn't know if their parents had even been rescued, and if they had been injured, how badly. She didn't want to get her hopes up only to be disappointed.

We often want to come up with solutions all by ourselves. We want to think of every way to solve a problem. But sometimes, we can mess it up.

The best way to solve a problem is to take it to God first. He always has the answer. If we commit our works or actions to Him first, He will establish our thoughts. That means he will give us the ideas and the plans for our lives.

When our life is devoted to God, He directs our thoughts and our plans. The devotion includes reading our Bible, praying, and being obedient to His Word. How we treat others is one way we display our dedication to God. The more we get to know God, the more we understand what He wants for our lives.

Sarah knew the first thing to do was to pray for guidance. She was eager to find out how God wanted her to proceed. And she showed godly wisdom when she asked her parents for permission.

✾ ACTIVITY

Write down how you show your devotion to God. What are some things God has shown you when you've asked Him to guide you? Ask Him today. He wants to establish your thoughts.

✾ PRAYER

Dear God, thank you for directing my thoughts and guiding me. Teach me to devote my life to You through Your Word and prayer. Amen.

"Hope deferred makes the heart sick;"

Proverbs 13:12 NLT

There was so much hope the day that Sarah, her parents, Sarge, Roman, and Daisy went to the animal shelter. They knew the rescued dogs were severely injured, but the possibility of finding Sarge, Roman, and Daisy's mom and dad and bringing them home would be an answer to prayer.

Imagine their despair when they finally looked around the shelter and didn't recognize any of the dogs. It made Sarge hang down his head in sorrow.

Have you ever felt such disappointment when you had hope for something that didn't happen? How did it make you feel? The Bible uses the word "sick;" "it makes the heart sick." That's not a very good feeling.

When something we hope for doesn't happen right away, or at all, it is "deferred;" which means it is put off, postponed, or delayed. There's that patient fruit again. Remember what we are to do when that happens – "Wait upon the Lord."

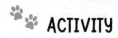 **ACTIVITY**

Write a story about a time you waited on the Lord.

35

 **PRAYER**

Dear God, so many things can make me disappointed
and sad. Thank you that even when I am sad and my
heart is sick, You give me courage and strength as I wait
on You, Lord. Amen.

"But a dream fulfilled is a tree of life."

Proverbs 13:12 NLT

Just when everything seemed hopeless for Sarah and her family, there was still one more chance! The most badly injured dogs were in a recovery room at the shelter. Special permission was needed to enter. Once they received permission to go in, it was only a matter of time before their dream would be fulfilled. It was a joy for Sarah and her parents to see Sarge, Roman, and Daisy reunited with their parents!

When hope is delayed, it makes the heart sick, but everything feels new when that hope comes true. Our heart leaps for joy and gives us new life! It restores our soul.

When was the last time disappointment made you feel sick, but then something incredible happened, and you felt well again?

Sometimes we don't appreciate feeling well until we've felt a little sick.

ACTIVITY

Write down something that you are hoping and praying for in your prayer journal. When your prayer is answered, go back and add that date next to it so you will remember when God answered your prayer.

37

 **PRAYER**

Dear God, thank you for always giving me something to hope for. So many times, it is beyond what I could ever hope for or imagine. May I always be grateful to You. Amen.

"The godly care for their animals, but the wicked are always cruel."

Proverbs 12:10 NLT

Sarge's parents had to recover before coming home and living with the rest of the family. Sadly, the men who stole them were cruel and abused the rescued dogs.

All animals are God's creation, and He gave us authority over them. Some animals provide us with milk or eggs, and some work on a farm. Many give us the meat we eat and enjoy. Pets, like dogs and cats, are animals that provide us with companionship.

Sarah took excellent care of her pets. She fed them and made sure they were safe and warm. She was a good steward of what God and her parents had given her.

ACTIVITY

Draw a picture of a fun time with your pet or someone else's pet you enjoy.

PRAYER

Dear God, thank you for making animals that not only feed us but provide companionship for us. Teach me to be kind to all of Your creation, not only animals but especially people. Amen.

SARAH'S Amazing ANIMAL ADVENTURES

A Series of Children's Stories About Character
Displayed Through Love and Kindness

Book FIVE

MEMORIES AND LOSSES

SALLY BETTERS
Illustrated by Linda Lloyd

Book 5 — Memories and Losses

"This is the day which the LORD hath made; We will rejoice and be glad in it."

Psalm 118:24 KJV

Thanksgiving, Christmas, and birthdays often bring back memories of happy times spent celebrating with family and friends. We look forward to those days.

When Sarah and her parents reunited Sarge, Daisy, and Roman with their mom and dad everything was joyful in their home. They ate together, played together, and laughed together. They went for walks in the park. It was a time of rejoicing. They were one big happy family. Think back on a wonderful day spent with family or with friends. What are some of the special moments you remember most?

When we know and love God, He prepares a place for us in heaven. A place where one day, a day the Lord has made, all those who belong to God's family will rejoice together with Him forever! God has prepared a day for us in heaven; don't miss out! Be glad!

 ## ACTIVITY

Write down what three things you are looking forward to in heaven.

 ## PRAYER

Dear God, thank you for each day of life. Thank you for the family and friends you've blessed me with. Teach me to be mindful of all Jesus has done for me so I will rejoice and be glad! Amen.

"For unto us a child is born, unto us a son is given: and the government shall be upon his shoulder: and his name shall be called Wonderful, Counselor, The mighty God, The everlasting Father, The Prince of Peace."

Isaiah 9:6 KJV

Sarah took some time to name her pets. She chose special names that represented their personalities. She named her new dog Aaron because its meaning described some of the qualities she saw in him.

What is your name? Does it have a special meaning? Some of us are named after a dearly loved grandparent, aunt, or uncle. Some names are passed down as a tradition. Some names are chosen because they are unique. Our name represents us. It identifies us. But how do we represent our name? What do others think of when they hear our name?

Jesus has many different names in the Bible. His name means "the Lord is my Salvation," and He definitely is our salvation because He came to save us from our sin. But He also has many names to describe his qualities: Wonderful Counselor, Mighty God, Everlasting Father, Prince of Peace, just to name a few. Those are some very amazing names and qualities to have and also a great way to remember who God is!

 ## ACTIVITY

Take some time to think about the name your parents chose for you. Sometimes the definition isn't as important as how you represent your name, and God wants us to represent Him by how we behave.

PRAYER

Dear God, thank you for loving us so much and sending your son, Jesus, to save us. Thank you that His name represents all that is good! Teach me to be an example of Your love so that when others hear my name, they will think of You! Amen.

"Turn your ears to wisdom, and concentrate on understanding."

Proverbs 2:2 NLT

Could Sarah really understand Sarge, Roman, and Daisy? Did she listen with her heart?

Since animals can't speak, it isn't very likely we will hear our pets talk to us in our language. But they can meow, cluck, moo, and bark when they are hungry, hurt, or want our attention. They can even warn us when danger is near. Some birds can even learn to repeat words they hear, and that is quite amazing!

We can get to know our pets by observing them and spending time with them, learning their habits and special traits even when they don't say a word!

If you think about it, that is how we get to know God! We can't see God, and we can't hear Him speak out loud, but He gave us a special book called the Bible. When we read it, we get to know who God is. In fact, He speaks to us through His words which are written just for us! We can incline (lean) our ear to hear his words as we read them, and if we listen with our heart, He will help us understand Who He is!

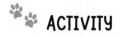 ## ACTIVITY

Spend some time with the Lord, reading His word and asking Him to give you understanding!

PRAYER

Dear God, thank you for the Bible that speaks to us and teaches us who you are! I want to spend time with you each day so that I can get to know you more. Thank you for loving me and taking good care of me. Amen.

The Lord says, "I will rescue those who love me. I will protect those who trust in my name."

Psalms 91:14 NLT

Who do you ask for help when you are troubled? Is it a friend, your mom or dad, or a brother or sister?

We usually talk to people we trust. However, we often feel alone, or maybe we are afraid to tell someone what is bothering us because we think they won't understand.

Sarge, Roman, Daisy, Aaron, and Iris are a family of dogs, but they share some of the same problems that people experience in these stories. They have a friend, Sarah, whom they trust, and they aren't afraid to tell her their troubles. Sarah is someone who cares and is ready and willing to help. a moment to think of some of the ways Sarah has helped her dog friends.

When we feel alone or afraid, there is a friend we can always trust and talk to; His name is Jesus. He is close to those who love Him, and He is waiting for us to call on Him. He loves us very much and is ready and willing to help. And He even wants to hear all about our good days! All we have to do is talk to Him through prayer. Isn't that wonderful? What a friend we have in Jesus!

ACTIVITY

Write down three ways you put your trust in God.

PRAYER

Dear God, thank you for sending Your son Jesus to save us! Thank you that through Him we can be closer to you. Thank you for hearing our prayers and are ready and willing to help us when things aren't going so well. Show me who the adults are in my life that I can trust; someone who can pray with me and encourage me to keep trusting in You. Amen.

"And God saw everything that He had made, and behold, it was very good..."

Genesis 1:31 KJV

Think of a beautiful day! The sky is a brilliant blue, and the trees are a vivid green. Maybe there is a lake close by, and the sun makes the water sparkle! The birds are singing cheerfully as you prepare a picnic with your family. These are the kinds of days we remember. And they are excellent days.

Sarah and her family spent many good days in the park surrounded by nature, enjoying each other's company.

When you look around, can you imagine how God might have felt after He created the sky, the sun, the trees, the birds, and the water, and YOU. And He calls it good! Very good!

 ACTIVITY

Next time you go outside, look around and name all the things you are grateful for about God's beautiful creation.

 **PRAYER**

Dear God, thank you for all that you have created, including ME! When I am outside, help me to enjoy the sights and sounds of your creation. Teach me to listen to the rain falling, the birds chirping, and the leaves rustling in the wind. Show me the flowers in the garden, and the moon as I count the stars and my blessings. It is good! It is very good! Amen.

"He maketh me to lie down in green pastures: He leadeth me beside the still waters."

Psalm 23:2 KJV

Sarah's days at the park with her family were filled with activity. There was also plenty of time for birdwatching while sitting on a comfy blanket eating and enjoying their surroundings. It was a time of rest.

Whether we work or play, our bodies get tired, and we need rest. Sometimes we become ill and we don't have any energy. Also, as we grow older, our bodies age and we become a little slower.

Iris was getting older and her body was feeling tired. Remember Iris and Aaron had not been treated well until Sarah's family adopted them, and now it was taking its toll on her body and she was sleeping more.

Thankfully, when we are tired or feel sick, God, The Good Shepherd, knows exactly what we need and where to lead us! He gives us rest. That's why He created our bodies to rest by sleeping or just being still. He can lead us to a place of safety, He can provide a bed for us to sleep in, or maybe He will lead us to a patch of grass under a shade tree (a pasture) by a lake (still waters) where we can lie down and relax. A place where we can rest in the Lord and have peace.

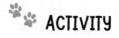 ACTIVITY

Tell your parents about an activity that makes you feel happy.

PRAYER

Dear God, thank you for making us rest when we are tired and weary. Thank you for leading us to peaceful places where we can sleep. Thank you, Lord, that we can rest in You and trust You to know what is best for us. Amen.

"He restoreth my soul: He leadeth me in the paths of righteousness for his name's sake."

Psalm 23:3 KJV

Iris had endured a very difficult time in her life when she and Aaron were separated from their pups and forced to work hard without rest or being properly fed. This caused her much heartache. But now, after her struggles, her joy has been restored. She is surrounded by her family and is being well taken care of. The love she was lacking has been restored!

When we endure difficulties in our lives, either by choices we've made or circumstances out of our control, we can feel defeated, lost, and broken. Only The Good Shepherd can restore us! He restores our souls! He forgives us if we've made a mistake and He rescues us by leading us on His "path of Righteousness" which is the path to Jesus. When we love Jesus with all of our heart, when we ask forgiveness, when we pray, when we spend time with Him reading our bibles, He restores our souls!

🐾 ACTIVITY

What kind of place or activity restores your soul? For Sarah, it was going on a picnic with her family and pets. Ask your parents if you can plan a fun event together.

 **PRAYER**

Dear God, thank you, Good Shepherd, for restoring my soul! Lead me each day to study Your word so I can remain on Your path of righteousness in the name of Jesus! Amen.

"Yea, though I walk through the valley of the shadow of death, I will fear no evil: for thou art with me; thy rod and thy staff they comfort me."

Psalm 23:4 KJV

Sarah received some very sad news from the veterinarian. She was about to lose Iris and it gave her a sad and sick feeling in the pit of her stomach. Aaron, Sarge, Roman, and Daisy were also aware that Iris would not live much longer. They never left her side. They wanted to make her as comfortable as possible so she wouldn't be afraid.

Sadly, losing a pet is usually one of the first experiences we have with death. We don't want to see our family pets suffer so we make an extra effort to comfort them so they don't feel alone. At the same time, we can be overwhelmed with sadness over saying goodbye to our furry friend.

When we fear death for ourselves or a loved one, it can feel like we are traveling alone through a very dark place. But The Good Shepherd is with us. He comforts us as He walks by our side so that we don't have to fear. He uses the rod to gently guide us to keep us from wandering from His path and His staff to protect us from harm.

Now that is very comforting!

ACTIVITY

Write down three things you are afraid of and ask God to help you with your fear.

PRAYER

Dear God, thank you for walking with me through difficult times. Thank you for guiding and protecting me. Teach me how to find comfort in You so I don't have to be fearful. Amen.

"Surely goodness and mercy shall follow me all the days of my life:"

Psalm 23:6 KJV

Now that Iris was gone, her family was left behind to mourn and remember. They cried and hugged each other. It was a very sad time. They missed Iris very much. This is called grief. One way they helped each other cope with grief was to remember Iris. They shared their favorite memories of her; memories that made them smile.

When we lose someone close to us, it can feel as though we will never be happy again. But The Good Shepherd promises that His mercy and goodness will follow us all the days of our lives. If that's true, then we know that we will be alright. Though we will not forget the one we lost, we can remember them with joy and gladness. God will restore our souls as He walks with us through the dark valley of grief because He loves us and His goodness will supply us with family and friends who will help us through our sadness.

ACTIVITY

Get a small journal or notebook and write down the good memories of someone you miss. When you feel sad write something good you remember about that person, it will help you to be grateful for the time you had together.

🐾 PRAYER

Dear God, thank you for your love and goodness. I pray that when I am sad over losing a pet or a loved one, You will help me remember the good memories of them and be thankful that they were part of my life. Teach me to appreciate the family and friends you have given me so that we can be a comfort to each other in times of need. Amen.

SARAH'S Amazing ANIMAL ADVENTURES

A Series of Children's Stories About Character
Displayed Through Love and Kindness

Book SIX

TAKING CARE OF LOVED ONES

SALLY BETTERS
Illustrated by Linda Lloyd

Book 6 — Taking Care of Loved Ones

"Honor your father and mother, which is the first commandment with a promise: that it may be well with you and you may live long on the earth."

Ephesians 6:23 KJV

Aaron's children display honor and respect by caring for him after the death of their mother, Iris. There are different ways we can honor our parents. A few ways are to obey them, show love and kindness, and take care of them when they are old.

Sarge, Roman, and Daisy took turns, along with Sarah, caring for their dad. They showed him love and concern for his broken heart and his painful hip. I believe it helped Aaron recover from the loss of his wife and the physical injury in his hip. Do you think having people you love take care of you will help you get well sooner?

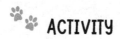 ACTIVITY

Write a note telling a loved one three things you love about them.

🐾 PRAYER

Dear God, help me to honor my parents and loved ones. I want you to teach me to take good care of my family and friends and show them the love you have shown me. Amen.

"Be kind and compassionate to one another, forgiving each other, just as Christ has forgiven you."

Ephesians 4:32 NIV

The famous author, Mark Twain, said, "Kindness is a language that the deaf can hear, and the blind can see."

In book 6, kindness and compassion are shown to Aaron by his children and Sarah while he is grieving the loss of his loving wife, Iris.

Kindness is more than being nice to someone and using your manners. It's a desire to show genuine love and compassion through your actions, words, facial expressions, and tone. It's a real concern that comes from your heart.

Aaron's children show him this love and compassion after their mother passes away. Sarah also shows great kindness in her tender care for Aaron by taking him to the veterinarian. In addition, she demonstrates her love and concern for Aaron by rubbing the pain cream in his leg to help him feel better.

There are many ways to show kindness to others.

🐾 ACTIVITY

Write down five ways you show kindness to others. Then make a list of people you would like to share your acts of kindness with.

🐾 PRAYER

Dear God, please show me new ways I can share kindness with others. Help me to share the love You have for them in simple ways. I love you, Lord! Amen.

"Let us consider how we may spur one another on to love and good deeds."

Hebrews 10:24 NIV

Sarah looks for activities that will include Aaron but will not be too tiring for him. For example, Sarge, Roman and Daisy took turns walking with their dad so he would not feel left behind. Aaron remained active and healthy because he was included in easy and fun activities.

Aaron was well-loved by Sarah and his children. They each made an effort to make him feel happy and welcomed. I believe their actions helped Aaron to heal from the loss of his wife and his injury.

 **ACTIVITY**

Do you have a friend or is there someone you know who doesn't have the toys, books, or lunch you enjoy every day? Think of a way you can share what you have with someone else.

PRAYER

Dear God, show me someone who is around me that I can share with. Thank you for providing for those in need. Amen.

"And do not forget to do good and to share with others, for with such sacrifices God is pleased."

Hebrews 13:16 NIV

Both Sarah and Daisy are thinking of ways to serve others. For example, Sarah makes jackets for her dogs to keep them warm, and Daisy wants to have puppies to bring joy to Grandma Grace's widowed friends. Both of these are sacrificial acts of kindness that show love and understanding.

Many people give of their time by making things or give money to help other people. It makes them feel happy to give to others.

There are always different ways to help someone else if we look for it.

ACTIVITY

If you have an animal, is there something you can make to keep them warm and safe?

PRAYER

Dear God, open my eyes to help me see the needs that are around me. Show me what I can do to offer love and kindness to someone else. Amen.

"A happy heart makes the face cheerful."
Proverbs 15:13 NIV

Sarah and Daisy are looking forward to providing puppies to Grandma Grace's friends. Can you imagine how much joy this gift will bring to those lonely ladies who have lost their husbands?

Puppies are known to bring great joy to anyone around them. But have you noticed that when someone has a new puppy, everyone wants to be around it and hold it? Maybe it's the warm, soft fur and sweet face, or it could be the cute bark and little tail that wags back and forth. Holding a new puppy is one of my favorite things to do. How about you?

ACTIVITY

Think of something that makes you happy. Tell someone you love what makes you happy and ask what makes them happy.

PRAYER

Dear God, thank you for all the things I have that bring me joy. Thank you for creating puppies so we can cuddle, love, and play with them. Amen.

SARAH'S Amazing ANIMAL ADVENTURES

A Series of Children's Stories About Character
Displayed Through Love and Kindness

Book SEVEN

NEW BEGINNINGS

SALLY BETTERS

Illustrated by Linda Lloyd

Book 7 — New Beginnings

"Rejoice with those who rejoice; mourn with those who mourn."

Roman 12:15 KJV

Sarah and her parents are excited about their new home. Sarah's dad got an upstairs office, and her mother finally received her dream of a craft room downstairs. From Sarah's bedroom window, she could watch her dogs play in the backyard, and it made her smile.

Sarah's grandparents came over often to visit and loved Sarah's family's new home. As time went on, Grandpa Paul became weaker and spent a lot of time in the hospital. Eventually, he died in the hospital, and Grandma Grace was very sad. Sarah's parents invited her over so she would not feel alone. Soon, the Abrams decided to have Grandma Grace move in with them to help her cope during this difficult time. This meant Mrs. Abrams would need to give up her craft room. She willingly did this to provide a place for her mother to live and feel safe and comfortable.

 **ACTIVITY**

Is there something you would be willing to give up so someone you love could feel loved?

 **PRAYER**

Dear God, help me to look for ways to share what I have so someone else can feel happy. I want to have a grateful and generous heart. Amen.

"I have given skill to all the craftsmen to make everything I have commanded you."

Exodus 31:6 NIV

Grandma Grace finds great joy in seeing her daughter and her granddaughter, Sarah, use the skills and talents of sewing to bring happiness to others. Mrs. Abrams used her sewing ability to make Sarah's clothes, and Sarah used her sewing skills to design and sew dog jackets for her dogs.

Grandma Grace never thought her skills of sewing military uniforms during the war would continue throughout future generations and bring a smile to others. When we use the gifts we have been given to bring joy to others, it fills our hearts as well.

ACTIVITY

Is there someone you know who has a skill that blesses others? Take a moment to thank them for what they do.

PRAYER

Dear God, thank you for all the gifts and talents you give to people to bring joy to so many. Help me to appreciate their abilities and let them know the value they bring to us. Amen.

"You are to bring into the ark two of all living creatures, male and female, to keep them alive with you."

Genesis 6:19 NIV

Sarah and her best friend, Amy, are thrilled that their parents gave them permission for Max and Daisy to have puppies. Daisy's body was growing bigger, and she was getting ready to give birth to the new puppies. There was excitement in the air, and Sarah stayed close to Daisy to make sure she had everything she needed. Finally, after nine long weeks, Daisy had a litter of five puppies. Sarah was with Daisy the entire time to provide comfort and care for her and the puppies.

Amy's family, Grandma Grace, and her two widowed friends all received the gift of wonderful new puppies in their lives. These small animals brought many happy days and lots of fun memories to their new owners.

 ## ACTIVITY

Ask someone you know who is a pet owner what their favorite things are about their pet?

 ## PRAYER

Dear God, thank you for all the wonderful, warm cuddly, and big funny animals you have made to bring us joy. Amen.

"May the righteous be glad and rejoice before God; may they be happy and joyful."

Psalm 68:3 NIV

This is truly a season of surprises for Sarah. Both she and Amy are thrilled to have new little pups around their homes to enjoy. Additionally, Amy is surprised and grateful that her parents decided to keep two of the puppies. Finally, both girls are thankful they live close to each other to visit the puppies and include the little dogs' parents.

Sarah surprises Grandma Grace with an adorable military dog jacket she designed, which reminded her grandma of Grandpa Paul's uniform when he was in the Marines. It was a joyful moment for Sarah and her parents to see Grandma Grace smiling from ear to ear with her new puppy she quickly named Shadow.

ACTIVITY

Can you think of a time that you did something for someone that made them smile with great joy? Tell someone about it.

Dear God, thank you for the sweet moments of watching someone receive a gift that brings them happiness. Amen.

"Since we live by the Spirit, let us keep in step with the Spirit."

Galatians 5:25 NIV

Sarah is amazed when she takes care of Grandma Grace's dog, Shadow, and her cat, Boots. While Sarah is talking with her dogs, Boots unexpectedly speaks up and wants to be a part of this private conversation. Sarah is shocked that Boots can speak and understand their conversation. This new wonder brought about a chance for all the dogs and cats to talk to each other.

Sarah showed Grandma Grace's pets great love and care, just like they were her pets. All of the fruit of the Spirit is displayed in Sarah's life as she shows great devotion to her family and her dogs.

ACTIVITY

Which one of the fruit of the Spirit do you think you have? Ask someone you trust which ones they see in you?

PRAYER

Dear God, thank you for giving us all the fruit of the Spirit so we can love other people better. Amen.

SARAH'S Amazing ANIMAL ADVENTURES

A Series of Children's Stories About Character
Displayed Through Love and Kindness

SHELTER
check-in

Book EIGHT

DOG JACKETS AND THE UNEXPECTED

SALLY BETTERS
Illustrated by Linda Lloyd

Book 8 — Dog Jackets And The Unexpected

"She opens her arms to the poor and extends her hands to the needy."

Proverbs 31:20 NIV

Sarah and her grandma were having a conversation while driving to the store. Grandma Grace noticed Sarah had a natural talent for designing and sewing dog jackets. She encouraged Sarah to take her hand-sewn gifts to other animal shelters to provide warmth and kindness for the lonely dogs.

Sarah consulted with her dogs, and they loved the idea! She was excited and took Sarge with her to buy more fabric to begin this dog jacket giveaway. Sarah used her talent to do good works, and she was rewarded by the appreciation of the animal shelter dogs and the workers.

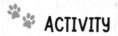 ACTIVITY

Is there something you enjoy making, drawing, or writing that will bless someone else? If so, take a step of faith and make something for someone else.

 **PRAYER**

Dear God, help me think of what I can do to bless other people, even if it's a small thing. Thank you. Amen.

"Therefore, as God's chosen people, holy and dearly loved, clothe yourselves with compassion, kindness, humility, and patience."

Colossians 3:12 NIV

Did you notice how patient and kind-hearted Joseph was when he met Sarah for the first time? He took a genuine interest in her compassion to help rescued dogs.

Sarah's well-dressed dogs displayed her care and thoughtfulness for animals. She included her pets in her visit to the shelter. Sarah wanted them to be included in her idea and to share the joy with them. She not only dressed her dogs well, but embraced the qualities of compassion, kindness, humility, and patience in her actions and attitude.

ACTIVITY

Do you relate to Sarah's heart and want to show compassion and kindness to others? What is one thing you could do to show others you care for them?

PRAYER

Dear God, thank you for the gifts you have given me. Show me new ways I can share them with others. Amen.

"Delight yourself in the Lord and he will give you the desires of your heart."

Psalm 37:4 NIV

Sarah's commitment to serving dogs in need was seen by her family, friends, and the animal shelter workers. Her desire to give jackets to the rescued dogs opened up opportunities to work at the shelter as a volunteer. Because of her kind heart in making and delivering dog jackets to needy dogs, Sarah was able to work at a place she loved, the local animal shelter, and learned more about how she could help the rescued animals.

New experiences and opportunities became available to Sarah as she committed her plans to the Lord.

ACTIVITY

Think about something you are interested in and ask God to give you ideas about how you can follow through with it.

PRAYER

Dear God, there are so many things I would like to do to help others. Please give me some specific ideas of what I can do today with what you have given me. Amen.

"Do not withhold good from those who deserve it when it is within your power to act."

Proverbs 3:27 NIV

Joseph took the opportunity to post the newspaper article about Sarah's Dog Jackets inside the Animal Shelter Lobby so everyone could see it. He also told Sarah how proud he was of her and the good things she was doing. This is an example of not withholding a good thing from someone else when it is in your power to do so.

Sometimes people don't want to give someone else credit for the good thing they are doing. This may be because they are jealous, but God has enough good things for all of us to do, so we don't need to withhold telling someone something nice when we have an opportunity to bring them joy.

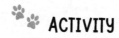 ACTIVITY

Is there someone in your life that you can tell what a good job you think they are doing? Take a moment to do so the next time you see them.

 **PRAYER**

Dear God, I want to do good things for others when you give me the opportunity. Please show me how and when to do them. Amen.

SARAH'S Amazing ANIMAL ADVENTURES

A Series of Children's Stories About Character
Displayed Through Love and Kindness

Book NINE

JOSEPH'S SECRET

SALLY BETTERS
Illustrated by Linda Lloyd

Book 9 — Joseph's Secret

"Therefore encourage one another and build each other up, just as in fact you are doing.
                                    1Thessalonians 5:11 NIV

Do you think both Joseph and Sarah are happy because they found a friend who loves animals, especially dogs? They shared a love of serving animals and each of them received great joy in watching the animals grow healthy and thrive. This foundation was a perfect beginning to a deeper relationship they would enjoy.

Both Joseph and Sarah are hopeful their friendship will allow them more time to work together at the animal shelter and on Joseph's farm. They enjoy encouraging each other to do the things that are important to them.

ACTIVITY

Have you hoped for something that has not happened yet? Write down your dream of what you hope will happen. Then, you can use what you wrote when you pray.

 **PRAYER**

Dear God, thank you for giving me ideas about things I want to do in my life. Help me to be patient and wait for your perfect time. Amen.

"Everyone enjoys giving good advice, and how wonderful it is to say the right thing at the right time."
Proverbs 15:23 TLB

Sarge is able to give Sarah good advice at the perfect time when her heart is breaking. Sarge knew Sarah needed to hear the truth about Joseph, but he needed to be sure Sarah was ready to hear it. His self-discipline and love for Sarah helped him to share at just the perfect time.

Because it was the right time, Sarah heard about Joseph's gift with animals, and she couldn't wait to talk with Joseph. Sarge's patience in waiting to share at the right time had huge benefits for his relationship with Sarah and Sarah's relationship with Joseph.

Waiting for the proper time to speak has many benefits.

 **ACTIVITY**

Has someone given you good advice at the right time that helped you? If you haven't thanked them, take the time to do it now.

🐾 PRAYER

Dear God, thank you for the people in my life who give me good advice when I need it. Help me to be thankful for them. Amen.

"May the God of hope fill you with all joy and peace as you trust in him, so that you may overflow with hope by the power of the Holy Spirit."

Romans 15:13 NIV

Sarah had a new hope after hearing Sarge share an important story about Joseph. It filled her with hope and joy as she trusted God for His plans for her life.

Because of her great joy, Sarah planned a special picnic for Joseph and her dogs. Sarah's fun surprise was a big relief to Joseph. Both she and Joseph were overflowing with hope about their gifts for animals and their growing friendship.

🐾 ACTIVITY

Do you have hope, joy, and peace because of the work God is doing in your heart? If so, write a letter to God and thank him.

🐾 PRAYER

Dear God, I am so grateful for all you give to me and the ways I can trust you. I want to overflow with your love for others. Help me show others that I am thankful for them. Amen.

"For I know the plans I have for you, plans to prosper you and not to harm you, plans to give you hope and a future."

Jeremiah 29:11 NIV

S arah's and Joseph's families have big parties to celebrate their children's graduations from high school and college. The families were thrilled to make a special event to celebrate their children.

It is a time to have a party and celebrate all the hard work Sarah and Joseph have done to finish their schooling. Both Sarah and Joseph have looked forward to this time and have plans for a bright future.

Were you surprised by Joseph's question to Sarah at his graduation party? They are trusting God will guide them as they seek God in all they do.

🐾 ACTIVITY

Do you ask God about things you want to do? Write down your prayers in a prayer journal and later add the date God answered them.

 **PRAYER**

Dear God, thank you for the hope you give us when we seek You for answers and direction for our lives. Please continue to direct my path in all I do. Amen.

"For this reason, a man will leave his father and mother and be united to his wife, and they will become one flesh."

Genesis 2:24 BSB

Have you ever been included in a big celebration, like a birthday or a wedding? It is such a great time of joy and excitement to celebrate with others.

This particular celebration was the beginning of new life for Joseph and Sarah. They would leave the homes where they were raised with their parents and start a new home together. Of course, they would take Sarah's dogs, Sarge, Roman, Daisy, and Joseph's dog, Walter, along in their new adventure.

God guided both Sarah and Joseph and fulfilled the desires of their heart.

ACTIVITY

Write about a time when you went to a wedding. Was it a fun time for you?

PRAYER

Dear God, help me to be joyful and celebrate with those who are having a special day. I want to be happy

for other people when good things happen to them.
Amen.

Join Sarah in the Series

SARAH'S Amazing
ANIMAL ADVENTURES

The heartfelt Sarah's Amazing Animal Adventures Series books by Sally Betters are remarkable tools for the emotional, physical, and spiritual wellness of children, parents, and families. Sarah's adventures with her dogs, Sarge, Daisy, and Roman, teach valuable lessons of love, kindness, friendship, believing in oneself, asking for help, and learning to look to God for guidance. Her chapter discussion questions and activity suggestions are creative and helpful aides for opening doors to communication and sparking the imagination.

Jean Voice Dart, Author/Coach/Teacher

www.jeanvoicedart.com

Read All

9 Books!

ABOUT THE AUTHORS

Sally Betters was born in East Los Angeles, California, raised in the suburb of Whittier, and earned a Liberal Arts degree from the University of California at Los Angeles.

Sally is a published author of the award-nominated nonfiction book, *From Crisis to Compassion.* Children and adults praise her successful debut children's book, *Looking Beyond the Sky*, and its accompanying coloring and activity book.

Sally lives in a quaint mountain community surrounded by pine trees, squirrels, rabbits, and deer. It is there she finds inspiration to write and lives with the love of her life, her husband: Richard. She is a devoted wife, proud mother of two amazing sons, a step-mom to a wonderful adult son and daughter, and a grandmother of five kind, loving, and intelligent granddaughters. Her passion for serving others with her skills, time, and talents shows through in her writing, speaking, and life coaching. You can contact Sally through her website at www.sallybetters.com.

Mary Jane Lopez resides in San Bernardino, California, with Steve, her husband of 38 years. Together they raised three daughters and a son and are the proud grandparents of six grandchildren.

Growing up, Mary Jane loved to write poetry and dreamed of one day writing children's books. Though God's path guided her steps in a different direction, the Author of her faith and the author of this book series graciously allowed her to contribute to this devotional.

ALSO BY SALLY BETTERS